Dr Steve Morlidge

THE LITTLE BOOK OF BEYOND BUDGETING

A New Operating System for Organisations:

What it is and Why it Works

Matador
9 Priory Business Park,
Wistow Road, Kibworth Beauchamp,
Leicestershire. LE8 0RX
Tel: 0116 279 2299
Email: books@troubador.co.uk
Web: www.troubador.co.uk/matador
Twitter: @matadorbooks

ISBN 997 81785899 287

British Library Cataloguing in Publication Data.
A catalogue record for this book is available from the British Library.

Printed and bound by CPI Group (UK) Ltd, Croydon, CR0 4YY
Typeset in 11pt Aldine401 BT by Troubador Publishing Ltd, Leicester, UK

Matador is an imprint of Troubador Publishing Ltd

MY NOTES

CONTENTS

FOREWORD

The concept of 'Beyond Budgeting' has been around for nearly twenty years now. Although it has helped transform many businesses and has become part of mainstream management thinking in some parts of the world, I talk to many business people who have still not heard of Beyond Budgeting. And many of those that are aware of it find the concepts difficult to grasp.

I believe that these ideas are too important to be overlooked or ignored – so I wrote this book to fill these gaps in awareness and understanding.

The name of the organisation itself gives some clue as to why these gaps exist. 'Beyond Budgeting' (BB) describes what it wants to get rid of but not what should take its place. Furthermore, the alternative that it advocates is not a simple blueprint that can be copied and rolled out across an organisation. Rather it is a set of principles that have to be interpreted in the context of the unique challenges and opportunities faced by any particular organisation

In addition, BB sounds like a small idea, of interest only to the Finance community. But in reality it is a large and subtle set of concepts that have important implications for the way that work is done and how organisations are structured and governed. To use an analogy from computing, BB looks like an organisational 'app' but it is more like an operating system; largely hidden from view but critically important to the functioning of the entire system and how it performs for its users: its employees, customers, suppliers and shareholders.

I have a lot of sympathy with anyone who struggles to get their head around these ideas because I have spent much of the last two decades getting to understand them myself.

My journey started in 1998 when, after a 20-year conventional finance career, I persuaded my employer (a large division of Unilever) to become one of the first sponsors of the Beyond Budgeting Round Table (BBRT), the research collaborative that gave birth to the concept. The experience of discovering how many companies had not only survived but thrived without the budgets that had made my work so frustrating and unfulfilling, transformed my life – well, at least my working life!

Over the course of the next few years I designed and led a Unilever-wide change programme based on BB, while serving as the European Chairman of the BBRT. This experience convinced me that these ideas really worked. And as the BBRT discovered more and more striking similarities in the ways pioneering companies had chosen to organise their affairs – without being aware of each other's existence – I became obsessed with trying to understand why; a quest that led me to a PhD in a branch of systems science. So when I left corporate life to promote these ideas more widely, I co-authored 'Future Ready', a practitioner's guide to business forecasting – an essential part of the toolkit practitioners need to transition from traditional budgeting. At various times along the way I convinced myself that I had a firm grasp on these ideas only to find that when I pulled on an intellectual thread the fabric of my thinking about how organisations worked unravelled, which meant that I had to start rethinking again.

It is only now, after many cycles of unlearning and learning, that can confidently say 'I understand'. And, like Marco Polo on his return from his journeys to strange lands, I feel compelled to share what I have discovered.

The book you hold in your hand is my best shot at communicating what I have learned in a simple way. It was originally an appendix to 'Present Sense' (a companion volume to 'Future Ready') – a book that explores the practical issues of measuring and communicating business performance without the false security provided by the fixed reference points of budgets and other arbitrary targets. But as I was writing, it became clear to me that it needed to be liberated – to become a guidebook for a wider audience who would otherwise not come across these intriguing and powerful ideas, or who might be sceptical or suspicious of a method that flies in the face of much conventional management wisdom.

In this short book I have attempted to chart the depth and breadth of the BB ideas and set out the implications for business performance and organisational life generally. I have avoided detailed or technical arguments, except where I thought it necessary to explain how everything fits together. I have used straightforward logic to describe the forces at work and to explain why BB is important for the organisation as a whole, not just those who are living through the frustrations of working with budgets first hand. And throughout I have avoided rhetorical arguments, not because I lack passion for these ideas, but because they can put off as many people as they inspire…and there are other authors who can do this better than me.

In summary, **my aim is to answer the question 'what is Beyond Budgeting?' in a clear and succinct way to help you make informed choices about the way that you run your business,** as an alternative to blindly copying your predecessors. The goal is to help you build more adaptive organisations, better able to meet the challenges and exploit the opportunities thrown up by the modern world.

Amongst the things you will discover are:

How the operating model used to organise and run the affairs of an enterprise impacts many aspects of corporate life, not just the level of business performance

The universal law of complexity that explains why traditional budgeting will always fail to deliver what it promises: predictable performance.

How the Beyond Budgeting process model is better equipped to deal with the complexity of modern organisational life and the uncertainty of the world

Why and how an organisation

has to be designed to complement the processes used to plan and control its activities.

How to bring about this change

I can't claim that this is the correct or authorised version of the BB model. It is simply a way of explaining it, based on what I have learned from working with these ideas over many years, informed by practical experience. Neither does the book answer the many 'how' questions you might have. Think of this as a guidebook of the kind that you would consult if you want to find out about a place or you are planning a trip there.

You will find some ideas on how to get started along with an inventory of some practical resources you will need 'on the road' at the end of the book.

Enjoy the trip.

Steve Morlidge

TWO STORIES

Not Again!

The post has just arrived and Gerry is as mad as hell. 'The nerve of it' she fumes.

In her trembling hand she has a letter from her bank. It coolly informs her that she has to pay an eye-watering fee for going over her overdraft limit for just a few hours. But what really enrages Gerry is that what took her over the limit was a charge generated by the bank itself – for a product the bank insisted she have as a condition of getting a mortgage…but that she didn't want. The final indignity is the administration fee the bank charged for sending the letter!

Later, after she has calmed down a little, she rings the bank's 'customer service' number. She dreads this task since she knows it will involve wrestling with an automated routing system and then listening to a nauseating mixture of Mozart and Lionel Richie on a loop for 20 minutes. Isn't it odd that whenever she phones to complain the bank's customer service centre seems to be experiencing 'very high call volumes'?

'If you stay in credit, your current account is absolutely free', the customer service operative unhelpfully says when Gerry finally gets through, obviously reading from a script.

'But you should be paying me. I'm lending YOU MY money!' Gerry replies.

Nothing in the customer service scripts seems to cover this point. 'Do you want to speak to my supervisor?"

A Different Experience

In another part of town Jim gets a phone call; it's his bank manager.

"Hi Mr Jones, it's Angela here, I've noticed that you have more money in your current account than you need to cover your scheduled payments; do you want me to transfer some to your savings account?'

It took some time for Jim to get used to receiving calls like this from his new bank after he had moved his account. At first he was suspicious; it even felt a little creepy after being neglected for so long by his previous 'service provider' – which is what his old bank claimed to be. Now it actually felt like his new bank cared about him. He even had the branch manager on speed dial. OK, so they charged a small monthly fee but this paid for itself whenever he asked for help, like the last time he applied for a loan and received personalised financial advice rather than a sales pitch.

'I could arrange a loan for you, Mr Jones' she said, 'but there is a risk that changes to the taxation of overseas interest could make this costly. I suggest you hold off for a few months until things are clearer, then perhaps we can talk through our fixed rate deals, which might be a better fit for your needs.'

What these stories tell us

Although I made up these stories, many more of us will recognise the first story than will have experienced the second – the poor service from traditional banks is only too real for many of their customers.

It makes us angry. And the UK banking regulator isn't too happy either.

In the period since the 2008 financial crisis, the regulator has fined UK banks over £7 billion for the misleading selling of a range of financial products to consumers and small businesses, ranging from protection against loss of valuables and identity fraud, through Payment Protection Insurance (PPI) and exotic interest rate swaps. In addition, the banks have been made to pay back over £20billion to customers in respect of PPI alone; equivalent to over £1,000 for every household in the country. And this is on top of the other huge fines they have paid to authorities around the world for manipulating benchmarks and facilitating money laundering.

The usual explanation given for this catalogue of misdemeanours is that the culture of banks is 'bad'. According to this narrative, the consistently dishonest behaviour from our banks is because they employ greedy sociopaths who only care about their year-end bonus. It may quell our sense of self-righteous anger to pin the blame on someone, but is this fair? Have you got any friends who work for a bank? Is that how you would describe them?

The second story is based on the experiences of customers of Handelsbanken, a Swedish bank that has been quietly but relentlessly growing their UK business. Handelsbanken do not advertise – there is no need because most of their customers have stories like the one we heard and who unsurprisingly recommend the bank to their friends. While other UK based banks were paying massive fines to regulators and trashing their reputations, Handelsbanken was increasing its presence from just a handful of branches to a network of over 200; advancing into the High Street at the same time as their competitors are retreating from it for cost reasons. At the time of writing the UK accounts for 10% of Handelsbanken's global profits, so somehow they

have managed to make money where other banks thought they could not.

Where does Handelsbanken find the paragons of virtue and rectitude that staff their branches? Other banks.

Handelsbanken recruit the people who we label greedy and unhelpful when they work elsewhere. Which raises the question: if 'the people' aren't the source of the problem with UK banks, what is? Is there some evil mastermind pulling the strings and making employees behave badly?

We all have a tendency to attribute the behaviour of the people we encounter to their personalities. In a simpler world, when business was more personal and conducted one to one, this might have been a useful shortcut for determining who to trust. But when we are dealing with modern complex organisations it leads us to look for the source of the problem in the wrong place.

The problem is rarely 'the people'; it is the system within

"The problem isn't 'the people'; it is the system in which they work."

which they work. So the solution doesn't involve 'working on the people' by exhortations to do stop doing the wrong things. Instead we need to uncover and change the processes, practices and structures that discourage people from doing 'the right thing'.

Financial News

September 2016

Problems mount at Wells Fargo: but who is to blame?

Yesterday Wells Fargo bank admitting to firing over 5300 staff over the last five years for unethical practices.

These include opening around 2 million phantom accounts for existing customer and transferring their money without their permission. The number of employees dismissed would make up the 16th largest bank in the US.

'This was a systematic attempt to meet production goals through the misappropriation of customer funds...this is a cultural issue and it needs a cultural fix'

Julie Ragatz,
Director of the Center for Ethics
The American College of Financial Services

A spokesman for Wells Fargo argued that it was a problem with a few bad apples...

'Instances where we provided a customer with a products that they did not request are totally counter to our culture and our values'

The boss was even clearer where the blame lay...

Unethical practices are often blamed on 'bad people' or 'the culture'...but is this diagnosis correct?

"The 5,300 were dishonest, and that is not part of our culture,"

John G Stumpf
CEO Wells Fargo
At Senate Banking Committee

A typical example of the mis-diagnosis of a systemic problem

THE HISTORY OF BEYOND BUDGETING

The Beyond Budgeting movement 'discovered' Handelsbanken in 1998, shortly after BB was set up in the UK. But the 'Handelsbanken way' was already well known in Sweden and to observers of the banking sector. Handelsbanken has never made a secret of the fact that their way of working didn't involve traditional practices like budgeting. They have described their approach to business in every financial statement they have issued since 1978, and often refer to it in other corporate communications. While Handelsbanken believe their success is a result of their methods, stock market analysts (who work for financial institutions rather like traditional banks) tend to be dismissive, calling them 'idiosyncratic' or 'old fashioned'. But in 1998 the Beyond Budgeting pioneers had a powerful motivation for wanting to dig deeper:

Were Handelsbanken's methods uniquely a product of their particular history, geography or culture?

Or were there hard and practical lessons that could be learned to make their model transferable to other companies, countries and industries?

In particular, we wanted to understand what exactly it was about their 'budget-free' approach that contributed to their spectacular performance across almost every important measure of business performance: customer service, employee satisfaction, consistent financial performance, stability and growth.

What we discovered was that Handelsbanken's success was not simply the result of their decision to abandon budgets in 1978. The Handelsbanken model was the result of a fundamental re-examination of the assumptions upon which traditional 'Western' management practice is based. And once we understood this and knew what we were looking for, we discovered that many other companies in other industries had independently come to similar conclusions about the best way organise and run their own businesses. This was clearly not the result of chance or a response to trends in thinking or fashion. All these 'BB' businesses had, through a combination of intuition and clear thinking, hit upon fundamental insights about organisations and how they should be run.

The key traits that all mature BB businesses shared, without exception, were flexible business planning processes and a devolved organisational structure, in place of the fixed annual budgets and functional hierarchies of traditional businesses. What was most interesting and unexpected was the range and nature of benefits that these businesses attributed to their way of working. Much more than you would expect if you thought "Beyond Budgeting" promised to merely to lighten the administrative burden.

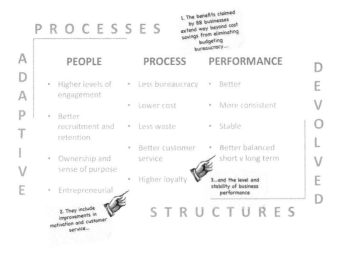

The benefits claimed by Beyond Budgeting organisations

Ultimately, the most powerful evidence comes from your own experience, and it was only when I personally witnessed the transformative impact of Beyond Budgeting ideas on the performance of a business that I had been involved with that I fully appreciated the power of these ideas.

To help share and promote these discoveries, the BBRT synthesised their learnings in a set of principles. But today, with the knowledge and understanding that comes from having worked with these ideas in practice for many years, I think we can do better. We can reveal the scientific logic that underpins the BB model to explain why and how

it works and so provide deeper insight and better practical guidance to implementers.

Like any journey of discovery, the best place to start is at the beginning; by exposing the foundations upon which traditional management models are built and so help you understand better how the BB model differs. First we will explore the processes used to plan and control financial resources. Then we will tackle organisational structure and governance and the implications of BB for the management of people and ideas before finally discussing how to start a BB journey.

"The key traits that all mature BB businesses share are flexible business planning processes and a devolved organisational structure."

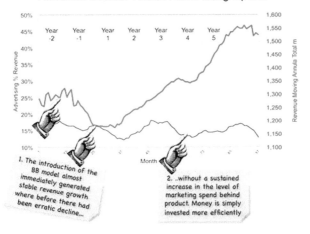

Revenue Growth versus Advertising Spend

An experience of the transformative impact of BB ideas in a subsidiary of a major Blue Chip company

THE TRADITIONAL PROCESS

Every traditionally run business manages its financial resources using a variant of a familiar routine:

Step 1: Build a Plan

The first step involves creating a set of business plans for the forthcoming financial year.

The plans are built on assumptions about the external world – what is expected to happen in the economy and how customers and competitors will behave. These plans also use a set of internal assumptions, such as the initiatives the business will take, how much resource they will consume and their impact on performance.

These plans can be produced 'bottom up'- with business units preparing plans which are submitted to the corporate centre for approval – or 'top down' where the centre issues high level targets which business units have to work back to – or a hybrid of the two. Finally they are added together to build a comprehensive plan for the total enterprise for the financial year.

In principle this approach is uncontroversial and sensible. But, in practice many versions of the plan are produced using different assumptions. As a result, particularly in large or complex businesses, we find that the process will be spread over many months and consume so much management time and attention that other business activities can grind to a halt. Perhaps the worst example I've come across was an international bank that admitted to spending 13-months each year preparing their annual plans!

Generating multiple, alternative business plans in this way costs time and money, but the problems really start at the next stage of the processes.

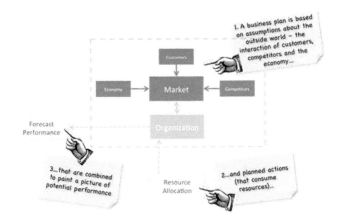

1. A business plan is based on assumptions about the outside world – the interaction of customers, competitors and the economy...

3...that are combined to paint a picture of potential performance

2...and planned actions (that consume resources)...

Build a plan

Step 2: Fix the Budget

After a prolonged period of debate and negotiation between managers and subordinates, the business adopts a single version of the plan that strikes a balance between what it assumes will satisfy shareholders and what it believes can be achieved, based on the perceived credibility of assumptions on which the plan is built.

This final plan is then locked in place and becomes the basis for the budget for the financial year. The budget is then broken down into fine detail and 'phased' over the quarters or months within the year because it is used as a reference point for performance analysis and to help co-ordinate actions across the business.

Despite the fact that it is only one of an almost infinite number of possible future outcomes, many of which may be more desirable, the final detailed budget is thus used as the basis for the planning and control of the business for the following year.

The outcome of the budgeting process is a detailed, interlocking set of constraints for a financial year. These take the form of targets for numerous output variables, such as profit or sales, and budgets for input variables such as investment and operating costs.

In practice, however, revenue and profit targets can act as a ceiling since there is no incentive to exceed them whereas cost budgets become a floor as there is no motivation to spend less.

" Revenue targets can act as a ceiling since there is no incentive to exceed them, whereas cost budgets become a floor as there is no motivation to spend less. "

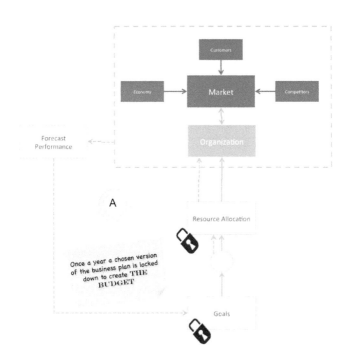

Fix the Budget

13

Step 3: Measure and manage performance

Over the course of the financial year control is exercised by comparing actual outcomes to the budget or target at a detailed level. The variance between an actual and the budget is assumed to represent good or bad performance, with managers expected to avoid or eliminate adverse variances (costs in excess of budget, or profit below target) by 'taking action' within the constraints of existing budgets.

In other words, the difference between the budget and the actual outcome is assumed to be the result of a combination of the effort and skill of managers. Consequently it follows that gaps can be closed by them 'performing better' or working harder, without the need for any changes in the allocation of resources. Little consideration is given to whether the assumptions on which the budget was based were realistic or, indeed, the inherent unpredictability of the world.

Often the budget also serves another purpose when they are used to construct 'performance contracts' with profit and cost centre managers. These are used to encourage people to 'hit their numbers' and to align behaviour with collective performance goals.

"The difference between the budget and the actual outcome is assumed to be the result of a combination of the effort and skill of managers... little consideration is given to whether the assumptions on which the budget was based were realistic."

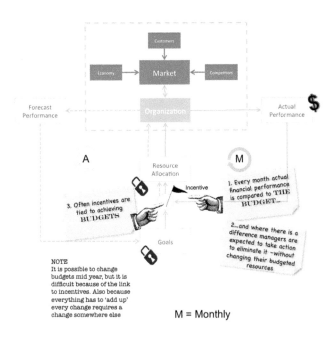

Measure and reward performance

In summary, a traditional budgeting system is made up of six tightly integrated key process components:

The Six Process Elements of a Traditional Budget	
Targets	Financial targets are fixed for a financial period and…
Incentives	Often tied to financial incentives. And…
Planning	Arrived at through a detailed annual planning process, which results in…
Resource Allocation	Investment budgets being fixed.
Measurement	Performance is monitored by analysing the variance between actual values and those in the phased budget, based on assumptions that performance should be managed back to plan, which, in turn, is based on the assumption that…
Co-ordination	Adherence to the plan ensures that the activities of different functions and business units are aligned so that collective performance goals will be achieved.

THE PROBLEM

The process used by most businesses today differs little from that first described in 1922 by James McKinsey in his book 'Budgetary Control'. Some advances have been made since then, especially in the use of IT to administer the process more efficiently. There are also nuances in the way different businesses implement budgeting, while management innovations such as Balanced Scorecard have broadened its reach. But none of these developments has fundamentally changed the basic architecture of the budgeting process set out nearly a century ago.

Budgeting might work well if it were possible to make well-founded assumptions about the future: if we were able to predict with confidence – twelve months in advance – what customers, competitors and the economy were likely to do, what decisions a business would make and what their impact would be and what external stakeholders would expect from the business.

The major problems with budgeting arise because we can't do any of these things in today's business environment – and we probably never have done. The interconnected nature of economies, businesses and customers makes their behaviour less predictable – and the task of anticipating the impact of decisions is even more difficult. Likewise, it is difficult to predict the needs of stakeholders because they base their judgements on the relative performance of the different organisations they could invest in, not on whether any one business has hit its own budget numbers.

'No plan ever survives contact with the enemy'

Helmuth von Moltke
Prussian Army Chief of Staff
'On Strategy' 1871

Businesses need to be able to change their plans to survive and prosper in an inherently unpredictable environment, but this is difficult with a budget in place. Because budgets have to 'add up', changing any one element will have a knock-on impact elsewhere, and any change will be resisted by those whose plans and pay are already 'locked in'. This is why adjusting budgets can be a time-consuming and fraught affair, even where the changes are relatively minor.

Budgets also sub-optimise performance by forcing the business to use the same set of numbers for competing purposes. On the one hand, good targets need to include an element of stretch, but forecasts need to be realistic, while cost budgets need to be 'tight' in order to constrain spending. It is simply not possible to fulfil all three purposes using the same number.

Finally, providing incentives for hitting budgeted targets (or taking sanctions against those who miss them) to motivate employees can have unintended consequences that run counter to the intended purpose.

Tying money to budgets almost inevitably leads to 'gaming' behaviour and suboptimal performance because it is in the financial interests of budget managers to negotiate targets that are easier to achieve. Finally, successfully focusing managers' attention on some targets by linking them to pay means those goals that are not, or cannot be, incentivised may be neglected, even if they are more important to the health of the whole organisation, such as maintaining high ethical standards.

Making a budget is an exercise in minimalization. You're always trying to get the lowest out of people, because everyone is negotiating to get the lowest number.

Jack Welch

In summary, budgeting is like a car that has been designed to operate only in ideal circumstances. As soon as it hits a bump in the road the wheels fall off. Why would you buy a car like that?

Problems with Traditional Budgeting	
Bureaucracy	The process of creating a detailed budget is inherently time consuming and costly…
Inflexibility	Making it inflexible and difficult to adapt to changing circumstances.
Sub-optimisation	Using the same number for competing purposes leads to the sub optimisation of performance…
Political	While using it for assessing performance and setting incentives encourages gaming behaviour (such as striving to negotiate lower targets and 'sand-bagging' cost budgets) and a focus on the internal affairs of the business rather than on markets or customers

These are simple, common sense arguments but there are more fundamental, systemic flaws in the traditional budgeting model. Understanding these will help us all to design better alternatives, so we need to dig a little further to understand something of the 'science' governing the management of complex systems. The key insights are enshrined in 'Ashby's Law of Requisite Variety', named after the systems theorist who first described them in 1956.

THE LAW OF REQUISITE VARIETY – A TOOL FOR MANAGING COMPLEXITY

Newton's Law describes how bodies with mass attract each other and so can be used to build better rockets by determining how much energy is required to escape the gravity of the earth. Ashby's Law of Requisite Variety (LORV) explains how complex, purposeful systems – such as businesses or organisms – interact with their environment. Ashby's Law helps us to isolate the systematic root cause of budgeting's problems and to design more effective processes.

Ashby's Law tells us that, in order to reliably achieve its goals, the flexibility of a control system (which is what budgeting is) needs to *at least match* the volatility of its environment. Because budgets are inflexible and the real world environment in which it is applied is unpredictable, this means that budgeting is incapable of fully achieving its intended purpose: to manage the performance of an organisation back to a large set of fixed targets.

Budgeting is designed to fail.

If you are happy to accept this assertion or if you find theoretical concepts boring you can skip to the highlighted paragraphs at the end of this section.

But read on if you are either sceptical or want to understand the fundamental principles upon which the design of *any* successful system of regulation must be based.

What Ashby's Law tells us may seem like simple common sense. But if it is, it is common sense that is widely misunderstood or ignored.

Where Newton's Law deals with mass, Ashby's Law uses a measure of complexity called variety. Variety describes how many states a system can adopt. For example, a heating system that can only be turned on or off has a variety of 2, whereas one that has 4 heat settings has a variety of 5 (off, plus the 4 'on' settings).

Ashby's Law describes the relationship between the varieties of three interacting systems:

First there is the environment. A stable environment has low variety; a volatile one has high variety.

Second there is the variety of the regulator or decision-making system. A system that provides a lot of flexibility has high variety (such as the heater with 4 settings) whereas one that has few control options (e.g. a heater with just an on or off switch) has lower variety.

Finally there is the variety of the objective or goal. Taking our heating system example, if we can tolerate a wide range of temperatures in our room we would have a high variety or 'loose' goal, but if we need it to be held within a narrow range we would have a low variety or 'tight' goal.

Ashby's Law is important because it allows us to describe what qualities a regulatory or decision making system (like budgeting) needs to be able to consistently achieve the goals of the organisation it serves. Expressed in simple terms Ashby's Law states:

The variety of the regulator

must be equal to or greater than:

The variety of the environment

divided by:

The variety of the goal

This tells us how much flexibility we need to build into a decision-making system (the requisite variety) if we are to meet our defined objectives in any given environment. For example, the range of control you need over your heating system is determined by how much the outside temperature varies and your target internal temperature range. The implications of the LORV for a heating system are obvious but the same principles also apply in much more complex situations.

For example, the regulatory variety of a sailing ship depends on the design of its hull, the number of masts and different sails it has, whether is has radar to enable it to sail at night or an auxiliary motor to enable it to move when there is no wind. It also depends on the crew – how many and how skilled they are. Whether the boat is capable of fulfilling its purpose depends on the variety of the environment: the range of weather and sea conditions that the boat encounters. It also depends on the goal: if it has to call at specific ports, at specified times to pick up passengers, the goal set has low variety, because the range of acceptable 'system states' is small, defined by a precise combination of time and place. If, on the other hand, it is on a lazy pleasure cruise with no particular aim in mind, its goal variety is high.

The mathematics underpinning Ashby's Law can become convoluted and in practice it is almost impossible to measure the variety of extremely complex real world systems. But while you cannot use the LORV to precisely engineer solutions in the way you can with the Law of Gravity, it is important to understand and respect it when you are designing organisational processes. A good design is one that consciously aims to balance the variety equation, as shown in the graphic overleaf. On one side of the scale there is the variety of the environment. This has to be balanced by the variety of the regulator plus the variety of the objective on the other side.

The importance of getting the design of the variety balance right is illustrated by what happens if the common sense principles of Ashby's Law are ignored – as they usually are with budgeting.

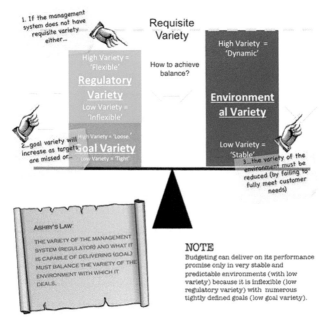

Balancing the variety equation

Budgets regulate the organisational system through the allocation of resources. This controls what can and can't be done, just as a heater switch controls the energy input into a room. Because budgets are prescriptive and fixed for a period of a year the regulatory system has low variety. The budget also defines the goal set – the system of targets – and this also has very low variety, because every element of the budget is broken down into quarterly or monthly targets that are used to measure and manage performance.

What Ashby's Law tells us about this situation is that it is only possible to meet all budget goals if the environment is highly predictable – if it too has a very low variety. If the environment is not predictable, the variety equation does not balance and something has to give way to restore equilibrium.

One thing that could 'give' is the level of environmental variety on the right hand side of the variety balance. Unlike our example of a boat and the weather, it is possible for an organisation to influence its environment; for example, choosing not to serve customers with complex needs can reduce environmental variety. You can also constrain their demands by narrowing the product range or by forcing them to use a low variety channel such as an automated telephone answering system.

If the variety of the environment isn't reduced Ashby's Law tells us that the variety on the left hand side of the balance **must** increase. There is no other alternative.

One way to restore the variety balance is to ignore (or fail to meet) some targets, since this increases the output variety of the system. In these circumstances, there is a high risk of prioritising those goals that are explicit, visible and tied to incentives, over those that are not, which may not necessarily be in the best interest of the business.

The only other way that the variety equation can be balanced is by adding variety to the regulatory system. Ideally flexibility will be built into the system, but if it isn't, people can create it for themselves by ignoring, bending or breaking the rules. Often the motives for not following the system are not malign and no harm is done. But if the stakes are high, deliberate 'law breaking' can prejudice the reputation or prosperity of the business, as illustrated by the mis-selling perpetrated by banks when employees are given very aggressive (low variety) sales targets.

To be clear, it is not necessarily bad for environmental variety to be constrained, or some targets missed – indeed, it may be unavoidable. The real problems start when the variety equation is balanced by accident, rather than design, and in a way that can negatively impact the organisation as a whole.

If these failings were recognised to be the result of a poorly designed system, the damage can be contained. Usually, however, the finger of blame is pointed at individuals or 'the culture in the business'. But no amount of punishment, exhortations to behave better, or even litigation can improve matters if the problem has been misdiagnosed.

None of this – the performance failure, poor customer service or bad behaviour – is necessarily the fault of any individual or groups of individuals working *within* the system. It is usually the fault *of* the system. If blame needs to be attributed anywhere, it lies with those who failed to design the system in line with Ashby's Law.

The Systemic Failings of Traditional Budgeting	
It ignores the nature of the environment	An annual cycle is used irrespective of the nature of the business environment.
It has low regulatory variety	The level of detail and the difficulty of making changes means it is difficult to respond to unanticipated threats or opportunities emanating from the environment or any other source.
It has low goal variety	The large number, specificity and fixed nature of targets

Like Newton's Law, the Law of Requisite Variety predicts what *cannot* work. Budgeting inevitably leads to suboptimal performance for the same reasons that having a centrally planned economy helped the Soviets lose the Cold War. But Ashby's Law cannot guarantee success. Designing a better system for running a business needs an understanding of how to apply the science, just as a successful space mission involves more than strapping thousands of tonnes of rocket fuel to a metal tube.

To apply Ashby's Law successfully the whole system needs to be designed and run in the right way.

AN ADAPTIVE, BEYOND BUDGETING PROCESS

Of course Jan Wallander, the man who designed Handelsbanken's business processes, didn't know about Ashby's Law, and James McKinsey was writing about budgeting over 20 years before it was discovered. Wallander's design was based on insights from his personal experience and the courage to trust his instincts and flout conventional wisdom. But while Ashby's Law can help us to understand the performance management system Wallander built in Handelsbanken, it doesn't mean we can simply copy what he did.

The key lesson I draw from my study of Ashby's Law is that an organisation's operating model should be designed around the nature of its markets and the way it chooses to compete within them – its organisational purpose. The way that an organisation is run needs to fit the niche in the economic environment that it is aiming to colonise, and its control processes should be tailored to circumstances rather than being bought 'off the shelf' or copied from a book.

> "An organisation's operating model should be designed around the nature of its markets and the way it chooses to compete"

So, an organisation's "operating system" should be designed from 'outside to in', not by using the 'copy/paste' button. But this does not mean starting from scratch. Pre-existing processes can be adapted, or you can learn from the experiences of others, which is the raison d'etre of the Beyond Budgeting Round Table. Guided by the BB principles and Ashby's Law you need to find a way that works for *your* business.

Inevitably then, implementing Beyond Budgeting is a journey of discovery without a predefined route, but it is helpful to have an idea of your likely destination before you set out. So let's paint a picture of a typical set of Beyond Budgeting processes – pointing out differences to traditional budgeting as we go along.

"Guided by the BB principles and Ashby's Law you need to find a way that works for <u>your</u> business."

Step 1: Measure Performance in a meaningful way

To understand the essence of Beyond Budgeting we need to start with measurement. Facts are real – but plans can be no more than informed guesses. Recognising that your ability to predict the future is limited, you must start by identifying those financial and non-financial variables that are most critical for the health of your business and then ensure you measure and analyse them in an appropriate way.

Most targets traditionally used to assess performance are set in a more or less arbitrary manner, but the comparators you *should* use will *ideally* be drawn from the environment, from the performance of peers, or good proxies for them. Your performance relative to your competitors and peers is why customers buy your products or services, or investors your shares, not whether you have hit an arbitrary internal target. In addition, because you share an environment with your peers, using relative measures sets performance in its proper context, based on actual rather than assumed business conditions.

In practice it can sometimes be difficult to source benchmark performance data that can be used for targeting, particularly that of competitors, in which case you will need to find good, surrogate goals. Also, while the extensive use of *measures* is key to a successful BB implementation, the number of *goals* should be restricted and, wherever possible, not fixed to a point in time – mindful of the constraints imposed by Ashby's Law.

"Your performance relative to your competitors and peers is why customers buy your products or services, or investors your shares, not whether you have hit an arbitrary internal target."

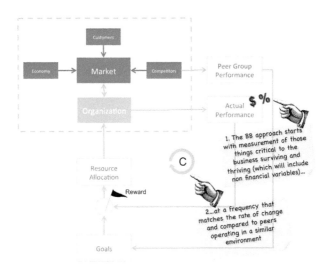

C = Continuous

NOTE
Information should be actionable, so start by identifying decisions that might need to be taken and then the data needed to support them

Measure performance in a meaningful way

Step 2: Forecast where required

Another consequence of Ashby's Law is that your measurement process should match the rate of change in the environment. In a fast moving market where you need to act quickly, you will need to update measures frequently. Handelsbanken publishes the performance of its branches every day and has the reflexes to respond quickly to this information, but few businesses are as nimble. Less agile businesses have to anticipate future outcomes, and so need to produce forecasts for the same reason that large ships need radar.

Predicting the future is inherently inexact, so you should always strive to increase your agility by reducing decision making lead times, accepting there may be limits to what can be achieved. For example, in the aircraft business it may take six months to build a plane, so a six months-out view will be required to steer the business reliably and to allocate your pool of scarce financial resources to best effect.

Although at first glace the forecasting process might look like budgeting, in practice it is very different because:	
The process is guided by the heartbeat of the business not an arbitrary financial calendar	Forecast horizons are tied to decision making lead times and are refreshed at the rate of change in the environment.
A forecast is never locked down.	Forecasts are constantly updated and the plans upon which they are based are locked down only when a commitment is made and resources irrevocably allocated
A forecast is an expectation whereas a budget is an aspiration	Its primary purpose is to identify gaps from target and so stimulate changes to plans

Step 3: Plan and Reallocate Resources Continuously

In BB businesses, resources are loosely attached to the plans upon which forecasts are based and, if the future is very uncertain, some may be held in reserve – unlike with budgets where resources are fully allocated when they are created. This means that when plans are changed, in response to events or a more compelling business case, resources can be easily reallocated. Funding is locked in place only when you decide to proceed, at which point resources are fully committed, **even if the project straddles a financial year-end.**

The frequency of the resource allocation process should also match the rate of change in the environment, rather than following an arbitrary financial calendar. This increases the agility of your business, while also, paradoxically, reducing the reliance on forecasts.

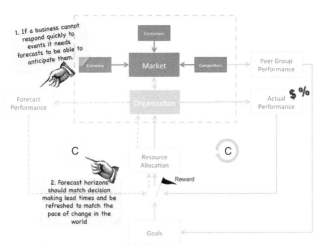

1. If a business cannot respond quickly to events it needs forecasts to be able to anticipate them.

2. Forecast horizons should match decision making lead times and be refreshed to match the pace of change in the world

Plan continuously and reward for shared success

Step 4: Reward Shared Success

The last piece in the BB jigsaw is the role played by remuneration.

BB businesses do not use traditional incentive systems because it is not possible to define meaningful targets in advance. In addition, they also believe that performance comes from people working together effectively, not from heroic individual efforts. Because of the level of interdependence within an organisation, the whole is always more than the sum of its parts. So, rather than using financial incentives based on a predetermined formula, the BB model rewards all employees based on a fair share of the wealth created by the business. This helps align collective behaviour around the organisational purpose.

In summary, the BB model performs all of the roles of a traditional budgeting system but in different ways. It generates targets and provides a framework for planning the future, allocating resources and measuring and rewarding performance. But instead of attempting to manage performance based on a single prediction of the future, the BB model provides the dynamic flexibility to adapt to the changing environment. The agility of their management processes helps explain the high performance achieved by BB businesses as well as the consistency of their returns – their responsiveness acting like springs absorbing bumps on the economic road. In Handelsbanken's case they have beaten the average return of their banking peer group for over 40 consecutive years.

Sometimes in business, you can just get lucky, but not 40 years in a row! The odds of this happening by chance are about 17 billion, billion to one.

Not bad for an 'old fashioned' business.

Processes: same ends - different means		
Purpose	Budget - Fixed	Beyond Budgeting - Adaptive
Target	Negotiated and fixed in time	Continuous and relative
Reward	Incentives based on target	Share in collective success
Plan	Predict and fix	Continuous anticipation
Allocate resources	Negotiate and fix	On demand based on context
Measure performance	Variance against target	Trends and alarms
Co-ordinate	Deliver on commitments	Dynamically synchronised

The BB story doesn't end here, however.

Budgeting plays a role in organisational life in ways that we have not yet touched on. The detailed plans underpinning budgeting help to co-ordinate activities right across the enterprise.

This need for co-ordination doesn't disappear when the BB process model is adopted. Indeed, because BB businesses have more flexibility, aligning organisational activity is more important and more challenging than for an organisation working with fixed annual plans.

Co-ordination is another sort of control problem, so we can apply Ashby's Law to help understand the implications. But this reveals a paradox.

THE ORGANISATIONAL PARADOX

By definition, organisations have to be organised. For them to function properly their activities need to be co-ordinated, aligned and synchronised. Without the cohesion this brings – if everyone did what he or she wanted to do when they wanted to do it – there would be chaos and the organisation would fall apart. In other words, *the flexibility (variety) of the organisation itself needs to be constrained* somehow. This is normally done by allocating roles, defining the relationships between them and the rules that govern decision-making across the business.

Traditional organisations are coordinated using a system of governance based on narrowly defined roles and functional silos set within a hierarchical structure. Decision-making authority is concentrated at the top of the organisation; a structure that neatly fits with budgeting. But this way of achieving alignment is at odds with the flexibility that BB provides.

All organisations need alignment, but some organisations and some situations demand more than others. Beyond Budgeting organisations need flexibility to adapt quickly to the *external* environment and because this implies a higher level of variety in their *internal* environment they are at greater risk of being uncoordinated than a traditional organisation using fixed budgets.

But this gives us a problem balancing a pair of apparently contradictory needs. How can we reconcile the need for flexibility with the need for organisational cohesion?

To restate the question using the language of Ashby's Law: how do we achieve the goal of effective alignment on the left hand side of the organisational variety equation (relatively low variety) while maintaining the internal flexibility we need on the right hand side (high variety)?

It is clear that traditional (low variety) systems of governance that tightly constrain employees activities are not consistent with a flexible approach to planning a business. To maximise the potential benefits of BB, businesses need a different system of governance – one that provides organisational cohesion without undermining the freedom to act.

In conclusion, in order to successfully make significant changes in the way that a business works it is important to treat processes, governance and structure as complementary interacting components of the organisation's operating system. A failure to take the whole system into account is why so many attempts to improve business performance by just restructuring the organisation chart or by changing isolated process elements fail to deliver the promised benefits.

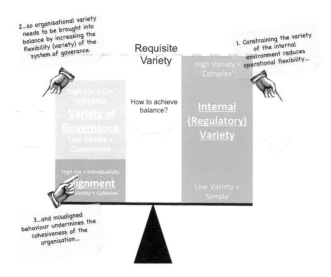

A paradox: Ashby's law and organisational design

THE TRADITIONAL HIERARCHICAL ORGANISATION

To answer the question 'how do we reconcile the need for flexibility with organisational cohesion?' we need a point of reference, so let's lay out the key characteristics of a traditional 'command and control' organisation of the sort that relies heavily on budgeting.

Structure	Roles are organised in a hierarchical fashion on the assumption that business as a whole will succeed only if everybody executes their part of the plan. Typically traditional organisations are structured along functional lines since specialisation helps them exploit economies of scale.
Governance	
Purpose	Although it might not be expressed this way on the plaque in the reception area, the business is organised to execute predefined plans effectively. In this way, the argument goes, it will be possible to consistently deliver returns to the owners of the business.
Authority	Decision making authority is concentrated in the hands of more senior employees because it is assumed that they are the most capable and best informed

Control	The organisation is controlled by ensuring that employees comply with the rules, procedures and policies associated with their role.
	Enablers
Information	Systems are organised to provide senior management with the information they need to make decisions and reassurance that performance is in line with plan.
Values	Power is concentrated at the apex of the organisation, so business performance is assumed to reflect the quality of the decisions made by the most senior executive and his or her ability to get them implemented. Employees are required to execute plans in line with procedure so their attention is directed inwards and upwards. In this world the boss is "King".

Although this simplified account doesn't reflect the nuances of real life, most traditionally run businesses co-ordinate their activities through some combination of concentrating power and a strict delineation of roles, supported by control and compliance mechanisms similar to those I've described above.

Where this _might_ work

There will be times in the life of every organisation when clear leadership and discipline are essential. For example, in emergency situations requiring swift and decisive action the hierarchical model can work well, particularly if the source of the threat and the actions needed to deal with it are easy to identify.

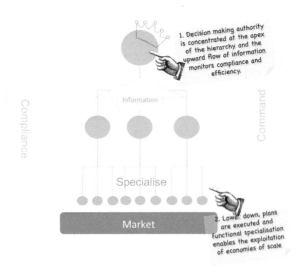

1. Decision making authority is concentrated at the apex of the hierarchy and the upward flow of information monitors compliance and efficiency.

Compliance

Command

Information

Specialise

Market

2. Lower down, plans are executed and functional specialisation enables the exploitation of economies of scale

How a traditional organsation works

Also, if employees do not have the information, skills or experience to make the right decisions on behalf of the organisation, 'command and control' may be the only way to go.

Where it doesn't

But if the environment is complex or dynamic, or if the centre is too far away from the action to make good decisions, and if those closest to the market are capable of intelligent independent action, the traditional hierarchical organisational model doesn't work so well.

In practice, in order to respond to the environment and meet the objectives that they have been given, enterprising employees will often ignore or break the organisation's rules to create flexibility for themselves, as predicted by Ashby's Law. In organisations managed through compliance, this behaviour is often not recognised to be a consequence of poor system design. Instead senior management redouble their efforts in response to these transgressions; reiterating the importance of ethical behaviour, creating more rules and introducing more monitoring. The end result is more bureaucracy, higher costs and the creation of ever more subtle ways of evading the new controls.

This kind of 'command and control' organisational model is sometimes described as 'regimented', but ironically, military thinkers realised long ago that they could not win wars with an organisation that works in a rigid 'top down' manner. Most land engagements since the First World War have been organised around small fighting units that are given freedom to make decisions for themselves – within limits.

Ashby's Law predicts the need for decentralisation of the kind practiced by modern armies when they are faced with a fast moving and unpredictable enemy. Over the course of the last century the military have learned how to design and manage their organisations in a way that enables decentralised decision making to be effectively co-ordinated in time and space. The key to maintaining alignment without compromising operational flexibility lies in building flexible – high variety – governance systems to replace the low variety bureaucracy of traditional hierarchies.

Faced with similar levels of environmental uncertainty BB organisations have also developed structures and systems of governance that are less hierarchical and more devolved than traditional businesses. These approaches reflect the unique and particular set of circumstances that each business faces. But, as we found with the BB process model, the solutions that the pioneering businesses hit upon have many defining features in common that provide a starting point and guide for anyone wishing to follow their lead.

Once the commander's intent is understood, decisions must be devolved to the lowest possible level to allow front line soldiers to exploit the opportunities available'

General Gordon Sullivan

A DEVOLVED BEYOND BUDGETING ORGANISATION

Beyond Budgeting organisations use a variety of complementary methods to build cohesion without undermining the operational flexibility they need to adapt to a dynamic environment.

Structure	Multi skilled teams are organised around the work that delivers value to customers in a well-defined segment of the market. Such teams are trusted with wide discretion to deliver against the purpose of the organisation but if they are not able to meet all the demands placed on them they can call upon centralised support units where people with special skills or capabilities are concentrated.
Governance	
Purpose	A clear and compelling mission for the organisation and how it is to be fulfilled (the strategy) helps employees orientate their actions in relation to the shared purpose while explicitly defined values and principles, describe how members of the organisation are expected to behave. In this way actions can be aligned without sacrificing flexibility and minimising the need for rules, regulations and central direction.

Authority	In order to maximise the range and speed of response, decision-making authority is clearly defined and delegated wherever possible. In this way decision-making is swift and well informed.
Control	Teams are held accountable for meeting broadly defined goals (their sub set of the corporate mission). Goals describe 'what' has to be achieved and the boundaries set by values and principles define 'how'. In this way BB organisations maintain cohesion without sacrificing operational flexibility.
Enablers	
Information	Free access to information creates transparency within BB organisations. This enables employees to self-organise with minimal central direction. It also creates the peer pressure that is a source of both personal motivation and the organisation's 'self control' by helping to build trust and by acting as a brake on dysfunctional or anti social behaviour.
Values	Beyond Budgeting businesses assume that success flows from serving the needs of customers better. Work is organised so that customers "pull" what they need from the organisation, rather than having the business force its agenda upon them. Employees are trusted to use sound judgement and act in the interests of customers and collective wellbeing rather than their own.

How this works

What all these characteristics of BB organisations have in common is that they create a framework that facilitates self-organisation. So, rather than being imposed, control is embedded *within* the organisational design and operates through 'self-control', supported by peer pressure.

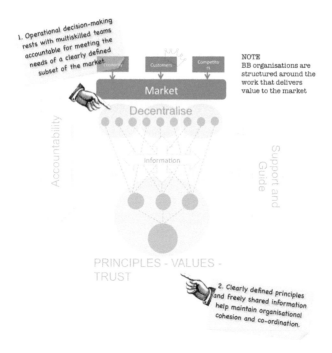

1. Operational decision-making rests with multiskilled teams accountable for meeting the needs of a clearly defined subset of the market.

NOTE
BB organisations are structured around the work that delivers value to the market

2. Clearly defined principles and freely shared information help maintain organisational cohesion and co-ordination.

How a devolved Beyond Budgeting organisation works

Principles, values, guidelines, goals and information combine to help individual members of the organisation make sound decisions, coordinate their actions with others and encourage them to 'do the right thing' within an environment based on trust. So what we call 'culture' is consciously co-opted into the control system of an organisation rather than being an accidental by-product of day-today interaction.

> "Rather than being imposed, control is embedded within the organisational design."

There are other possible 'high variety' governance methods that can be used to reconcile the need for both alignment and flexibility.

Rules and procedures could be modified to allow more flexibility, in the same way that exceptions and provisos are written into national tax codes, for example. Alternatively a centralised function could be given responsibility for co-ordination. For example, the complicated logistics of a distribution operation demands a high degree of co-ordination that is unlikely to spontaneously evolve and so central involvement is required to build the necessary infrastructure.

But such alternative approaches should be specific responses to well-defined needs, rather than an overarching administrative framework. These kind of mechanisms can become legalistic or bureaucratic, particularly in a complex environment, and thus more costly and less effective than a system that relies primarily on self-regulation. So more formal co-ordinating mechanisms should be used 'surgically' in a targeted way to avoid the centre becoming over-mighty or bloated. The need for

cohesion needs to be consciously and continually balanced with the need for autonomy.

Reasons to believe

These ideas may seem idealistic or impractical but there are striking similarities with the way that other types of social organisations have evolved in response to their increasing complex environments.

As already mentioned, following the catastrophic experience of the First World War, characterised by the grand plans and timetables of centralised military bureaucracies, modern armies are based on small cohesive teams that self-organise on the battlefield around the commanders intent and rules of engagement. Their training equips them to deal with a wide range of scenarios without recourse to higher command and radio communication enables them to co-ordinate their actions with their peers and call for back up when needed.

Following centuries of rule by absolutist monarchies, western liberal economies now function with minimal central direction, guided by the principles of democracy, liberty and the rule of law. Most economic and social intercourse is based on trust while the justice system and the activities of a free press constrain deviant behaviour without the need for every citizen to be subject to detailed rules and continual compliance. Price mechanisms provide the information that enables suppliers to organise themselves to meet the needs of customers. So instead of the command and control of planned economies we have principles and values, checks and balances.

The similarity between these different types of organisation and those upon which Beyond Budgeting is modelled is not accidental. It is the inevitable consequence of Ashby's Law and the evolutionary pressure of centuries of dispute, debate and competition. Beyond Budgeting provides organisations with a set of guidelines to enable them to consciously organise themselves to meet the challenges of today's complex economic reality, rather than having the brutal logic of the market force change upon them.

"Beyond Budgeting provides organisations with a set of guidelines to enable them to consciously organise to meet the challenges of reality, rather than having the brutal logic of the market force change upon them."

THE BB PRINCIPLES

The process and organisational perspectives are summarised in the 12 Beyond Budgeting principles.

Over the life of the BBRT there have been subtle changes in the wording and there are nuances in the way that different people interpret them; but the core message has been consistent.

Beyond Budgeting	
from command & control to empower & adapt	
Leadership principles	
1. Purpose – Engage and inspire people around bold and noble causes; *not around short-term financial targets*	**4. Organisation** – Cultivate a strong sense of belonging and organise around accountable teams; *avoid hierarchical control and bureaucracy*
2. Values – Govern through shared values and sound judgement; *not through detailed rules and regulations*	**5. Autonomy** – Trust people with freedom to act; *don't punish everyone if someone should abuse it*
3. Transparency – Make information open for self-regulation, innovation, learning and control; *don't restrict it*	**6. Customers** – Connect everyone's work with customer needs; *avoid conflicts of interest*

Mangement Processes	
7. Rhythm – Organise management processes dynamically around business rhythms and events; ***not*** *around the calendar year only*	**10. Resource allocation** – Foster a cost conscious mind-set and make resources available as needed; ***not*** *through detailed annual budget allocations*
8. Targets – Set directional, ambitious and relative goals; ***avoid*** *fixed and cascaded targets*	**11. Performance evaluation** – Evaluate performance holistically and with peer feedback for learning and development; ***not*** *based on measurement only and* ***not*** *for rewards only*
9. Plans and forecasts – Make planning and forecasting lean and unbiased processes; ***not*** *rigid and political exercises*	**12. Rewards** – Reward shared success against competition; ***not*** *against fixed performance contracts*

As the principles make clear, Beyond Budgeting is neither a tool nor a methodology. BB plays a similar role in an organisation that the operating system does for a computer. It is vital for the performance of the system, but largely hidden from view. Like an operating system, the BB model sits in the background but determines which organisational 'apps' can be run and how much value they deliver for the organisation.

Two of the most important organisational 'apps' involve the management of people and operational business processes.

IMPLICATIONS FOR PEOPLE AND LEADERSHIP

It should be clear by now that Beyond Budgeting has a different 'theory of people' to the one that underpins the traditional approach to control.

An organisation that relies heavily on rules and compliance is one that believes that its employees cannot be trusted. And if actions are driven by decisions imposed from above the implicit assumption is that they are not competent to make them for themselves. Tying personal financial incentives to the achievement of predefined outcomes assumes that people are motivated purely by money and that the success of the entire business is a simple sum of individual achievements rather than the result of effective teamwork.

These assumptions may be correct! If your employees are untrustworthy, incompetent and greedy they need to be policed, told what to do and managed with both carrot and stick. And some organisations are individualistic, relying very little on teamwork.

But if your world is not like this then at best you are imposing costly and unnecessary bureaucracy on your employees, at worst you help create an environment of distrust that can foster unhealthy attitudes and behaviour, while stifling innovation.

On the other hand, because of its reliance on self-organisation, a Beyond Budgeting organisation needs people that are trustworthy, competent and motivated by the desire to do the 'right thing' out of professional pride and a sense of personal fulfilment.

In BB organisations money is used to recognise the contribution made to collective success not as an incentive for individuals to act in a particular way, and is allocated based on principles of fairness. Because personal traits are critical to the success of Beyond Budgeting, such organisations focus on recruiting people with the right attitude since skills can be more easily taught. And crucially, any breach of trust or betrayal of values must be swiftly and clearly dealt with because they are the bedrock on which the model is built.

Similarly, leadership in BB companies takes a distinctive form. While decisive action and difficult choices will still be needed on occasion, leaders primarily act indirectly by setting the strategy, coaching, guidance and most importantly by modelling the behaviour that they want to see in their colleagues. This contrasts with the traditional 'heroic' business leader who makes the rules and calls all the shots.

"Any breach of trust or betrayal of values must be swiftly and clearly dealt with because they are the bedrock on which the BB model is built."

IMPLICATIONS FOR OPERATIONAL PROCESSES

The Beyond Budgeting model provides an operating system based on adaptive processes and devolved decision-making to help organisations respond effectively to their environment and mobilises the energies and talent of their workforce. The Beyond Budgeting model doesn't <u>manage</u> performance; it <u>enables</u> performance by providing the infrastructure that allows businesses to operate in more efficient and effective ways than is possible with a conventional command and control operating system.

An illustration of how BB provides a platform for value-generating processes is the way that it supports so called 'Lean' approaches to the management of production or service delivery.

Traditional western process management is based on exploiting economies of scale.

This often involves creating large, specialised units focused on part of a process that, because they are decoupled from upstream and downstream processes, rely on demand forecasts to plan their operations. This approach aims to drive down unit costs for each sub process. But it can actually result in higher costs in total because the difficulty of predicting demand and large lot sizes often leads to high levels of inventory or poor customer service – or both at the same time.

'Lean' and similar approaches used in the service sector avoid these problems by building a delivery system that provides the customer with what they want, when they want it.

By creating a 'pull' system, where supply flows are synchronised with the rate of demand, inventory and other forms of waste can be designed out of the system. A zero waste philosophy, coupled with a rigorous approach to continuous improvement (Kaizen) – harvesting marginal gains wherever and whenever they can be found – often leads to lower units costs than a traditional 'push' system built with cost in mind. And because it is designed around the needs of the customer rather than those of the organisation, it can provide spectacular service at the same time, as the stories we heard at the start of this book illustrate.

The BB model perfectly complements 'flow' process management because both employ an outside-in approach. And BB also facilitates Kaizen because continuous improvement cannot be planned in the conventional sense. Resources need to be made available to make changes wherever and whenever an opportunity is spotted unconstrained by planning cycles. Waste reduction targets cannot be set in advance and no master timetables can direct the process – a degree of flexibility that BB organisations can easily accommodate. For the same reasons, BB also provides a fertile environment for other management methods that place a premium on flexibility, like 'agile' software development.

With conventional budgeting on the other hand, 'improvement' targets and the resources needed to deliver them are 'hard coded' into the plan so there is limited scope to provide additional resources over and above those originally negotiated even if the other opportunities present themselves.

"The BB model doesn't <u>manage</u> performance it <u>enables</u> performance."

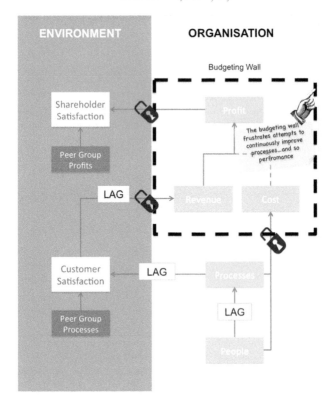

How the budgeting 'wall' frustrates process improvement

Budgeting effectively builds a wall around the financial variables of the organisation, and the gates through this wall are firmly locked most of the time. This 'budgeting wall' makes it difficult to make changes to the investment made in processes or the people that run them. Indeed, if the cost of an investment of any sort falls in one financial year but the benefits accrue in the next, cutting these projects is an easy way to 'hit the profit number' when the pressure is on towards the end of the financial period – so budgets actually become the enemy of improvement.

GETTING THERE

So how has budgeting survived for so long given its shortcomings and given how much the world has changed since it was conceived?

One of the reasons why people find it difficult to change a budget-based operating system is that its various components fit together like the bricks in a wall. The fact that everything 'adds up' is part of its intuitive appeal. The coherence of budgeting, which makes it rigid and inflexible, can also make it difficult to 'budget better' by making pragmatic incremental improvements. For example, it is difficult to reduce the level of detail in the budgeting process if you continue to use traditional variance analysis to analyse performance.

However, the fear of undermining the integrity of the whole system by changing one of its component parts is unjustified. In practice, it is possible to proceed incrementally without the roof falling in. For example, demonstrating that it is possible to change the way performance is measured or to decouple the setting of targets from forecasting without losing control, makes it easier for a business to take the next step towards BB. But proceeding 'one brick at a time' can be a slow process, requiring constant vigilance to ensure that budgeting and the mentality associated with it does not reassert itself over time.

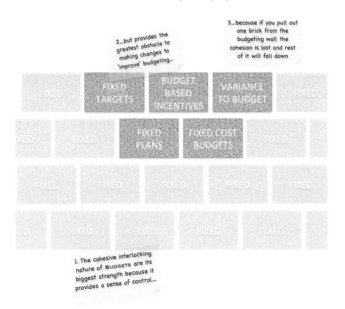

3...because if you pull out one brick from the budgeting wall the cohesion is lost and rest of it will fall down

2...but provides the greatest obstacle to making changes to 'improve' budgeting...

1. The cohesive interlocking nature of BUDGETS are its biggest strength because it provides a sense of control...

The biggest obstacle to change: the budgeting wall

For this reason some people believe that making changes to budgeting demands a full frontal assault on its walls with battering rams and siege engines. To succeed, they argue, you need a big inspiring vision and a charismatic individual to lead the charge.

The gradualist and fundamentalist approaches are sometimes presented as mutually exclusive alternatives, but I think they lie on a continuum. However diligently you work at scraping away the mortar between the bricks of the budgeting wall it is unlikely that it will collapse under the weight of its own contractions – at some point it will require a push to bring it tumbling down. Similarly, even after a 'BB revolution' there will be a lot of work involved in unpicking old practices and fashioning new ones. After nearly half a century even Handelsbanken still describe themselves as being on a journey.

In practice, the nature of the challenges faced by a particular organisation at a particular time and the art of the possible are what determine the best approach to take to bringing about change. There are only two things that we can be sure of.

First, when adopting this approach the benefits increase exponentially as your implementation becomes more complete, coherent and mature. Any change from traditional budgeting will add value but it may take some time before your new 'way of working' becomes a source of competitive advantage.

Second, before embarking on a journey of change you need to know what success looks like and in what direction you should head to find it. Also your chances of reaching your goal are improved enormously by persuading other people to join you on the journey.

"The nature of the challenges faced by a particular organisation at a particular time and the art of the possible determine the best approach to bringing about change."

GETTING STARTED

I hope this is a path that you want to tread. If it is, I hope that this book has given you a clear sense of what can be achieved, sufficient knowledge to help recruit others to your cause, a clear idea of the challenges that you will face and the confidence to make a start.

Your recruitment strategy needs to be crafted for your own particular audience, but to ensure that the message you use is effective it needs to contain enough of the four key ingredients.

1. Dissatisfaction

Anyone impacted by the changes you want to bring about needs to be unhappy with the current situation before they will join you. Their dissatisfaction might be to do with the business -perhaps its level of performance, or the way that it works – but it could also be very personal. For example, the impact of budgeting on the working lives of those that administer the process or those on the receiving end can provide powerful motivation for change. Anyone just starting out on their career has a particularly big stake in a better future but those already in a position of power might feel frustrated by a failure to make a real difference in their career. Any or all of these can be the source of the dissatisfaction that provides the fuel for change.

2. Vision.

You also need to paint a picture of a brighter future to enrol people on the journey. Since your own organisation's journey is unique, and you want other people to contribute, it may not be possible to describe the hoped for future in detail. But you need to paint a picture that is credible and made tangible; so the experience of other businesses that have made similar changes is critical to building confidence. Most important though, the vision needs to be inspiring since it is only by engaging the hearts as well as the minds of a large number of people will you unleash the energy and creativity you need to succeed.

3. First Steps

The tension between an unacceptable current reality and an inspiring vision of the future creates the potential for change but this energy needs to be channelled in a practical way. However good our maps, we cannot anticipate everything that you will encounter on your journey so it is not possible or necessary to build a comprehensive implementation plan. There will always be surprises, good as well as bad. But before you start you must have a clear idea of what first steps you will take, ideally those that provide some 'quick wins' to help you recruit supporters and build momentum.

4. Resistance

No matter how compelling your case for change, there will always be some resistance. This might come from those who stand to lose something – status, job security or the power and financial rewards that come from being good at playing the 'budget game'– but it could also come from less tangible sources – fear, uncertainly or doubt. Whatever the sources of potential resistance it is important to either bypass the obstacle it represents or weaken its power by confronting it directly at an early stage of the journey; ignoring it will only hasten its growth.

To bring about change you need to use each of these ingredients, but everybody will combine them differently to create their own recipe. It is particularly important to remember that, however powerful the rational argument is for change, often the most effective way of mobilising support involves an emotional appeal, a visual demonstration or an appeal to personal experience.

To get you started here are examples of the kind of questions you can use to help you create your own change manifesto.

Dissatisfaction: some questions to ask the organisation...

- How much time is consumed in the process of creating budgets: in finance and in the business?
- How long is it before the budget becomes out of date?
- How easy is it to change budgets to reflect changes in circumstances?
- Are opportunities missed because of budget constraints?
- Do people build slack into their cost budgets?
- Is there a mentality of "use it or lose it" with respect to cost budgets towards the end of the year?
- During the budget process do people try to negotiate low targets that are easier to achieve?
- Do people slacken off once targets have been achieved?
- Do people manipulate activity to hit targets at period ends?
- Are people ever praised or blamed when it is clear that the target setting process is at fault?
- Do important long-term projects ever get stopped to hit period end targets?
- Do budgets ever get in the way of serving customers or improving processes?

Vision: what if...?

- Everyone had the freedom and capability to do the right things for customers and the business?
- Employees were self-motivated self-starters, leaving leaders free to lead?
- There were no limits placed on improvement and achievement?
- Success was celebrated but falling short invoked support not blame?
- Good ideas could come from anywhere at any time?

- Energies were focused on beating the competition not hitting the number?
- Work was both fulfilling and fun?
- Adapting plans to changes was pain free and quick?
- Red tape and bureaucracy were slashed?

First Steps: consider...

- If budgeting didn't exist how would you set targets, allocate resources, measure performance, forecast performance, co-ordinate actions and reward good performance?
- How can process components be decoupled to loosen up planning and control across the business?
- Is it possible to experiment with new operating configurations in part of the business?
- How do we build and maintain the capability to plan, deliver and sustain transformational changes in organisational processes, structure and culture over a prolonged period of time?

Resistance: how can the barriers to change be lowered?

- How do we deal with those whose roles or status could be threatened by change?
- What can we do to manage the risk that some changes will not succeed?
- How do we deal with sceptics, inside and outside the business?
- How can we minimise uncertainty when we don't know what the future holds in detail?

AND IN THE END...

This book started with a story about two banks, told from a customer's perspective. We saw how one of these banks applied BB principles to create a way of working that enables them to provide excellent customer service <u>and</u> spectacular financial performance. Their methods are not, as their detractors argue, idiosyncratic, old fashioned and unprofessional, but a manifestation of sound scientific principles applied in a sophisticated and rigorous manner.

Once the logic underpinning their approach is exposed it is clear that, despite its name, Beyond Budgeting is not just about budgets at all. It provides deep and powerful insights into the nature of organisations. It teaches us to think differently about management; how the processes and structures we build shape collective behaviour and how this behaviour is translated into business success.

Our century old legacy management model is a product of the early years of professionalised management but the Beyond Budgeting model provides us with a coherent 21st century alternative better suited to the 21st century challenges faced by businesses. How to grow but keep costs down? How to perform consistently when the world will not stay still? How to access the resources that come with scale while remaining sensitive to the needs of customers? How to reconcile the human need for autonomy with organisational cohesion? How to embrace the complexity of the world and the need for simplicity?

This is good news. The less good news, as I and many others have discovered, is that once you understand this it may become difficult to work in an organisation where these ideas are not understood or practiced. It is also difficult to resist the temptation to become a Beyond Budgeting evangelist. High-minded preaching can be off-putting, and not just to those who disagree with you. It is also possible to miss the fundamental point that what is important are the principles and what they represent, not the form that they take, and in the process alienate potential allies who advocate a different manifestation of the same kind of ideas.

The history of management theory is told as a competition between incompatible ideas. Schools of thought grow up around self-appointed gurus whose words are taken to be the sole and definitive source of knowledge by their followers. And after their death their disciples take up the cause, fighting self-righteous battles against rival groups with the most bitter conflict often being between those who share many of the same views.

Advocates of BB should be wary of dogmatism. We cannot lay claim to 'the truth'. We simply describe a way of working that is in tune with the world in which we live, with human nature and with universal principles. I believe the real power of Beyond Budgeting is not its uniqueness but in its resonance with many other modern management ideas and its ability to remove the biggest barrier to their successful implementation. This is what I think 'Beyond Budgeting' really stands for.

I see the role of BB advocates captured in a story told by the Indian mystic Osho. He describes a Japanese Buddhist temple that contains just one object: a statue of a finger pointing upwards.

"It is a finger pointing to the moon. All words are just fingers pointing to the moon, but don't accept the fingers as the moon. The moment you start clinging to the fingers – that's where doctrines, cults, creeds, dogmas, are born – then you have missed the whole point. The fingers were not the point; the point was the moon."

FURTHER READING

A personal selection of important sources of reference, support and inspiration.

The Fountainhead Seminal books in the life of the Beyond Budgeting movement	
Beyond Budgeting: How managers can break free from the annual performance trap Jeremy Hope & Robin Fraser Harvard Business School Press (2003)	The original Beyond Budgeting book, based on the research of the founder members of the movement
Decentralisation – Why and How to Make it Work: The Handelsbanken Way Jan Wallander SNS Förlag (2003)	A description of the principles and practice of Handelsbanken by its architect. The most important source of inspiration for the Beyond Budgeting model.
Practical Support Some sources of practical guidance for implementers.	
Implementing Beyond Budgeting: Unlocking the Performance Potential (second edition) Bjarte Bogsnes Wiley (2016)	Based on the experiences of a serial implementer of BB in two major companies

Future Ready: How to master business forecasting Steve Morlidge & Steve Player Wiley (2009)	A practical guide to improving forecasts as a means of breaking the stranglehold of budgeting on performance management.
Present Sense: A Practical Guide to the Science of Measuring Performance and the Art of Communicating it – with the Brain in Mind. Steve Morlidge In progress 2016	Describing practical alternatives to traditional variance analysis and tabular presentations based on exploiting the brain's sense making capabilities.

Supporting Literature

Books written by members of the movement in support of the BB approach and philosophy

Beyond Performance Management: Why, when and how to use 40 tools and best practices for Superior Business Performance Jeremy Hope & Steve Player Harvard Business Review Press (2012)	A series of books exploring different aspects of performance management with BB principles positioned centre stage
The Leader's Dilemma: How to build an empowered and adaptive organization without losing control By Jeremy Hope, Peter Bunce & Franz Röösli Jossey-Bass (2011)	
Reinventing the CFO: How financial managers can transform their roles and add greater value Jeremy Hope Harvard Business Press (2006)	

Fellow Travellers

Books written by advocates of complementary, non-traditional methods in related fields of management

Out of the Crisis W. Edwards Deming MIT Press (2000)	A devastating critique of traditional practices by a guru of the Quality movement.
The Toyota Way: 14 Management Principles from the World's Greatest Manufacturer Jeffrey Liker McGraw-Hill (2004)	A description of the practices and philosophy of the company that has been the model for most recent innovations in manufacturing, misleading labeled 'Lean'.
Freedom from Command and Control: A Better Way to Make the Work Work John Seddon Vanguard Consulting Ltd (2003)	A description of the destruction wrought on service management by traditional practices and how to avoid it by an advocate and practitioner of Deming's methods

Sources of Inspiration

Books that describing an inspiring complementary vision of alternatives to traditional management practice.

The Living Company: Habits for Survival in a Turbulent Business Environment Arie de Geus Harvard Business School Press (1997)	A veteran Shell senior executive explores the importance of treating businesses as organic entities with purpose, dependent on and contributing to their environment, rather than managing them as machines.

Relevance Regained: From top-down control to bottom-up empowerment Thomas Johnson The Free Press (1992)	Two books that trace the intellectual journey of a self confessed 'recovering cost accountant' from a position of managing by ends (fixed targets) to managing by means (doing the right thing, better)
Profit Beyond Measure: Extraordinary Results through Attention to Work and People H. Thomas Johnson & Anders Bröms Free Press (2001)	
Reinventing Organizations: A Guide to Creating Organizations Inspired by the Next Stage in Human Consciousness Frédéric Laloux Nelson Parker 2014	Studies of companies successfully breaking many of the old rules about the way organisations should be structured and run.

Contact me

If you want to buy multiple copies of this book for friends or colleagues or if you are interested in creating a special customised edition of this book for your organisation contact me at steve.morlidge@ satoripartners.co.uk

I would welcome your comments and suggestions about this book – positive or negative.

WANT TO KNOW MORE?

The Beyond Budgeting Institute is at the heart of the movement that is searching for ways to build lean, adaptive and ethical enterprises that can sustain superior competitive performance. They promote a set of principles that lead to more dynamic processes and front-line accountability. Organisations that follow this approach transform their management model in line with these principles.

The ideas are spread through the Beyond Budgeting Round Table (BBRT); a shared learning network of member organisations with a common interest in transforming their management models to enable sustained, superior performance. BBRT helps organisations learn from worldwide best practice studies and encourages them to share information, past successes and implementation experiences to move beyond command and control.

The BBI works through a global network of local partners – typically consulting companies – that help organisations make the change.

If you want more information about Beyond Budgeting and the BBI can help, you can contact them here:

Beyond Budgeting Institute
One Kingdom Street
Paddington Central
London W2 6BD
United Kingdom
Tel: +44 20 3755 3692
Mail: info@bbrt.org
Web: www.bbrt.org

THANKS

The Beyond Budgeting idea has enriched my life for nearly two decades and I owe an enormous debt of gratitude to the people I have met through the community. Two of its original leaders – Jeremy Hope and Peter Bunce, have sadly been taken away from us far too early, but they retained their enthusiasm and their enormous generosity of spirit right to the end. Happily, one other founder, Robin Fraser, is still going strong and continues to work on these ideas, and Anders Olesen has picked up the baton and leads the community with the same energy, openness and integrity.

I have met many other wonderful people through the community who I would also like to thank. In particular, Steve Player has been my partner on various Beyond Budgeting adventures over the years and Bjarte Bogsnes of Statoil has probably more experience than all of us put together and remains a source of inspiration and an example of courage and dedication for all us – myself included. Steve and Bjarte are still involved in the community – in the US and Norway respectively – working alongside many other great people including Dag Larssen (Sweden), Franz Roosli (Switzerland and Germany), John Seddon (UK) and Axel Guðni Úlfarsson (Iceland).

I have learned an enormous amount from all these guys, but this book is very much my take on Beyond Budgeting, so I take full responsibility for any errors and failings. If you are confused or annoyed by anything that you have read I am sure that any of them would be happy to hear from you so that they can correct my mistakes!

ABOUT THE AUTHOR

Dr Steve Morlidge is married to Sue and has three grown children and a small white dog.

He is a management thinker, speaker and writer and is also a founder of CatchBull Ltd, an innovator in forecast performance management software, mainly for the supply chain community.

He lives in the Surrey countryside, south of London.